WORLD OF INSECTS

Grasshoppers

by Emily K. Green

BLASTOFF! READERS 2

BELLWETHER MEDIA • MINNEAPOLIS, MN

Note to Librarians, Teachers, and Parents:

Blastoff! Readers are carefully developed by literacy experts and combine standards-based content with developmentally appropriate text.

Level 1 provides the most support through repetition of high-frequency words, light text, predictable sentence patterns, and strong visual support.

Level 2 offers early readers a bit more challenge through varied simple sentences, increased text load, and less repetition of high-frequency words.

Level 3 advances early-fluent readers toward fluency through increased text and concept load, less reliance on visuals, longer sentences, and more literary language.

Whichever book is right for your reader, Blastoff! Readers are the perfect books to build confidence and encourage a love of reading that will last a lifetime!

This edition first published in 2007 by Bellwether Media.

Library of Congress Cataloging-in-Publication Data
Green, Emily K., 1966-
Grasshoppers / by Emily K. Green.
p. cm. – (Blastoff! readers) (World of insects)
Summary: "Simple text accompanied by full-color photographs give an up-close look at grasshoppers."
Includes bibliographical references and index.
ISBN-10: 1-60014-014-9 (hardcover : alk. paper)
ISBN-13: 978-1-60014-014-3 (hardcover : alk. paper)
1. Grasshoppers–Juvenile literature. I. Title. II. Series.

QL508.A2G745 2006
595.7'26–dc22 2006005334

Printed in the United States of America.

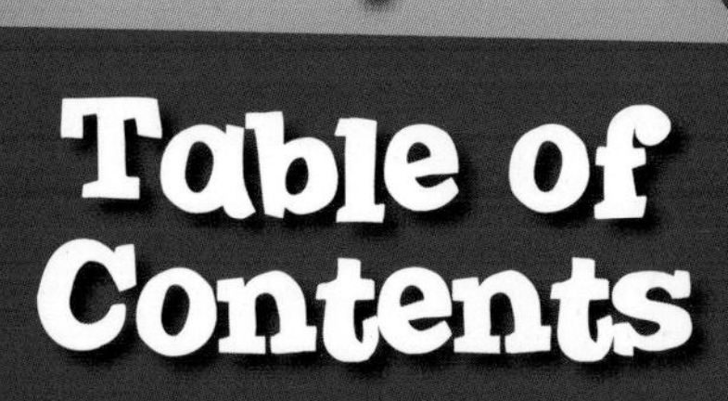

What Is a Grasshopper? 4

How Does a Grasshopper Look? 6

What Does a Grasshopper Do? 14

Glossary 22

To Learn More 23

Index 24

Grasshoppers are **insects**.

Grasshoppers live everywhere on Earth except in really cold places.

All grasshoppers have two **antennas**. They use their antennas to smell and feel.

Some grasshoppers have long antennas.

Some grasshoppers have short antennas.

A **locust** is a kind of grasshopper with short antennas.

All grasshoppers have six legs. Their back legs are strong.

Grasshoppers use their back legs to jump.

Most grasshoppers have four wings. Their front wings are straight and thick.

Grasshoppers use their back wings to fly.

Most grasshoppers **chirp**.
Grasshoppers use their
wings to chirp.

They rub their wings together or they rub one leg and one wing to chirp.

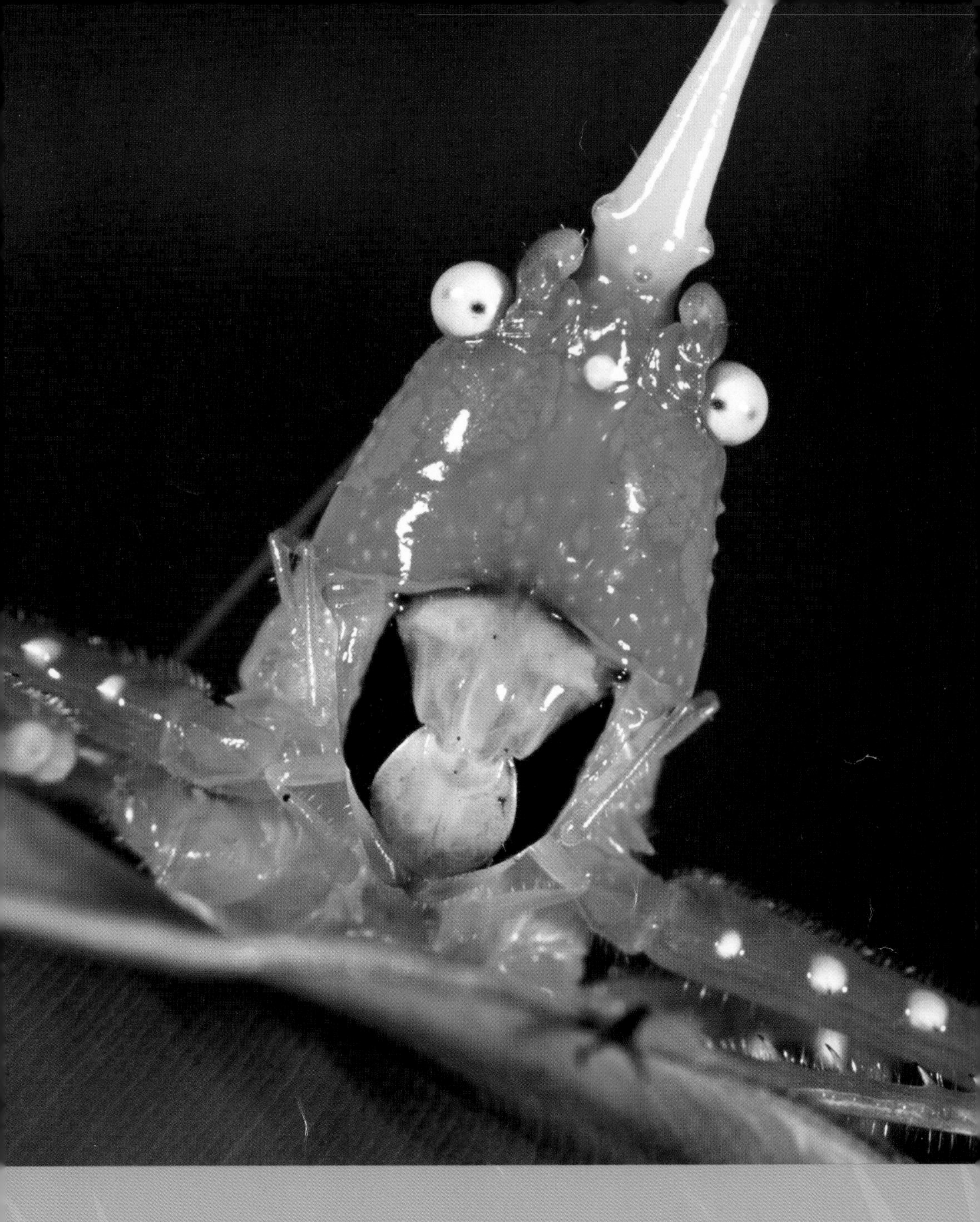

Grasshoppers can hear.

A grasshopper's ears are on its legs or on its **abdomen**.

Grasshoppers eat grass and other plants.

Grasshoppers use their strong **jaws** to chew.

Sometimes many grasshoppers fly in a group called a **swarm**.

A swarm of grasshoppers can eat all the plants in this field.

Glossary

abdomen—the back part of a grasshopper's body

antennas—the long, thin feelers on an insect's head; grasshoppers use the feelers to touch and smell things.

chirp—the short, buzzy sound that a grasshopper makes

insect—a kind of animal that has a hard body; most insects also have two antennas, six legs, and two or four wings.

jaws—part of a grasshopper's mouth; a grasshopper chews food with its jaws.

locust—a kind of grasshopper with short antennas; locusts are also called short-horned grasshoppers.

swarm—a large group of insects that move around together

To Learn More

AT THE LIBRARY

Allen, Judy. *Are You a Grasshopper?* New York: Kingfisher, 2002.

Barner, Bob. *Bugs! Bugs! Bugs!.* San Francisco: Chronicle Books, 1999.

Lobel, Arnold. *Grasshopper on the Road.* New York: Harper and Row, 1978.

Loewen, Nancy. *Hungry Hoppers: Grasshoppers in Your Backyard.* Minneapolis, Minn.: Picture Window Books, 2004.

Williams, Sheron. *Imani's Music.* New York: Atheneum Books, 2000.

Zuchora-Walske, Christine. *Leaping Grasshoppers.* Minneapolis, Minn.: Lerner, 2000.

ON THE WEB

Learning more about grasshoppers is as easy as 1, 2, 3.

WWW.FACTSURFER.COM

1. Go to www.factsurfer.com
2. Enter "grasshoppers" into search box.
3. Click the "Surf" button and you will see a list of related web sites.

With factsurfer.com, finding more information is just a click away.

Index

abdomen, 17
antennas, 6, 7, 8, 9
ears, 17
Earth, 5
field, 21
grass, 18
group, 20
insects, 4
jaws, 19
jump, 11
legs, 10, 11, 15, 17
locust, 9
plants, 18, 21
swarm, 20, 21
wings, 12, 13, 14, 15

The photographs in this book are reproduced through the courtesy of: Luis Castaneda, Inc./ Getty Images, front cover; Tony Alt, pp. 4, 19; Andrew F. Kazmierski, p. 5; fl online/Alamy, pp. 6-7; Marcus Gosling/Alamy, p. 8; Thylacine, p. 9; National Geographic, Dr. Darlyn A. Murawski/ Getty Images, p. 10; Dwight Kuhn Photography, p. 11; david & starr/Getty Images, p. 12; Premium Stock/Getty Images, p. 13; Florida Images/Alamy, pp. 14, 15, 17; Olivier DIGOIT/Alamy, p. 16; Andrea Gingerich, p. 18; Carl D. Walsh/Getty Images, p. 20; Oleg Prikhodka, p. 21.